LUV-ALL
(0-0)

ACE LIFES GAME: MASTERING TENNIS VALUES TO ENHANCE ESSENTIAL LIFE SKILS.

Siddarth Bellalcheru

Copyright © <2024> <Siddarth.Bellalcheru>

Made with ❤ on the Notion Press Platform

www.notionpress.com

Contents

Preface

At the tender age of 4, I picked up a tennis racket for the first time, unknowingly embarking on a journey that would define much of who I am today. Now, at 16, tennis is not just a sport to me—it is a way of life, a mirror reflecting the struggles, triumphs, and lessons that shape my existence. The path has been anything but straightforward; it has been a rollercoaster ride filled with exhilarating highs and humbling lows, each moment carving a deeper understanding of the game and life itself.

From the early days when the court felt impossibly large, and the rules were a mystery, to the present, where every shot, every decision feels like second nature, my journey in tennis has been a series of evolving challenges. Growing up on the court, victories brought a fleeting euphoria, while defeats often lingered, casting long shadows over my confidence. Yet, within these shadows, the most profound lessons were learned.

My parents and coaches have been the guiding lights in my journey. They taught me to see beyond the immediate outcomes of a match. Wins were celebrated, of course, but it was in the losses that the real work began. They instilled in me the belief that every defeat was not a failure but a chance to learn, to grow, to come back stronger. This mindset, though difficult to embrace at times, became the cornerstone of my development as both a player and a person.

The dinner table became a sanctuary on those challenging days when a match didn't go as planned. It was here that my parents, with their unwavering support, helped me dissect every aspect of the game. We would analyze what went wrong, celebrate what went right, and, most importantly, discuss how I could improve. Each loss was transformed into a lesson, fueling the fire within me to train harder, refine my skills, and prepare for the next challenge.

As I started competing in more tournaments, I noticed a puzzling pattern. Some opponents I easily defeated in practice became formidable adversaries in official matches. Conversely, players who once bested me became more accessible to overcome in subsequent encounters. This inconsistency gnawed at me, leading to countless hours of introspection. Was it just my technique that was lacking, or was there something more?

Through candid conversations with my coach and parents, I began to uncover the truth. The issue wasn't just with my physical game but my mental game. I had overlooked the psychological aspect of tennis, which, as I would soon discover, was just as critical as technical skill. My mother, a behavioural expert and psychologist, played a pivotal role in this discovery. Together with my coach and father, they helped me explore the mental aspects of my game, unveiling a new dimension of tennis that I had previously ignored.

Initially, I was skeptical. I questioned the necessity of focusing on mental health when my physical abilities seemed sufficient. But as I began to develop this aspect of my game consciously, the results spoke for themselves. I realized that envisioning myself as x times better than my opponents was an unsustainable approach. Instead, I needed to understand how the mind and body work together to achieve peak performance.

This journey led me to delve deeper into the World Health Organization's life skills and their application in tennis. What started as a quest to improve my game evolved into a broader exploration of how these life skills influence not only sports but also various facets of daily life. The connection between mental resilience, emotional control, and success on the court became clear, and I knew this story was worth sharing.

This book is the culmination of that journey. It is a reflection of my experiences, a collection of insights gathered from interviews with coaches, professional players, and friends. It offers a comprehensive understanding of how life skills shape a tennis career, and how the lessons learned on the court can be applied to life off the court as well.

I extend my deepest gratitude to the coaches who guided me, the fellow players who challenged me, and the friends who supported me throughout this enlightening journey. I hope this book serves as a guide, providing a holistic perspective on the intricate dance between life skills and the exhilarating game of tennis. Whether you are a seasoned player, a beginner, or someone simply looking to understand the connection between sports and life, may you find value in these pages and be inspired to apply these lessons to your own journey.

Important Note

In this book, the context is set within the world of tennis, a sport that has been my personal classroom for learning and applying the ten core life skills recognized by the World Health Organization (WHO). Tennis, with its demands for strategy, precision, and mental fortitude, has provided a unique perspective on how these skills—self-awareness, empathy, critical thinking, effective communication, interpersonal skills, decision-making, problem-solving, creative thinking, stress management, and coping with emotions—can be developed and honed.

However, it is crucial to understand that these lessons extend far beyond the boundaries of tennis. While my experiences in this sport have been the foundation for these insights, the principles discussed are applicable to any sport, cultural event, or personal hobby. Each skill can be viewed and applied broadly to enhance various aspects of life. Whether you are engaged in a different sport, participating in cultural activities, or pursuing a personal interest, the life skills explored in this book are designed to improve your overall well-being and effectiveness in diverse contexts. These insights are not limited to the realm of tennis but are valuable tools for personal growth and success in any area of life.

Acknowledgments

I would like to express my deepest gratitude to my mom, a behavioral psychologist, whose insights and expertise shaped much of the content on life skills in this book. From the very beginning, your understanding of human behavior and emotional intelligence served as a foundation for this work. You not only helped me with the content but also patiently explained the deeper significance of each skill, showing me how they extend far beyond the tennis court and into everyday life. Your thoughtful feedback, whether it was a suggestion for a chapter or a detailed review of the entire manuscript, ensured that every word was carefully considered. You always encouraged me to think critically and reflect deeply, not just as a tennis player but as a person learning from every experience. I owe much of the clarity in this book to your dedication and love, and for that, I am forever thankful.

To my dad, whose idea it was to embark on this journey of writing—there aren't enough words to express how much your belief in me has meant. From the moment you suggested the idea of writing a book, you've been my biggest advocate. You taught me that tennis, like life, is a journey filled with wins and losses, and it's how we respond to those losses that truly defines us. Your perspective on viewing every setback as an opportunity to learn has become one of the most important lessons I've carried with me. You've always been there, not just for the victories but, more importantly, during the moments of doubt. Whether I was frustrated after a tough match or struggling to find the right words for a chapter, you were the one who encouraged me to keep pushing forward. Your late-night pep talks, countless hours of support on the sidelines, and relentless motivation have kept me going through the toughest times. You reminded me that the journey of both tennis and writing is filled with ups and downs, but persistence is what leads to true growth. Your unwavering belief in my potential has been the fuel behind everything I've accomplished, and I couldn't have done any of this without you.

To all my coaches, past and present, thank you for pushing me beyond my limits, for believing in my potential, and for playing a key role in my growth as both a player and a person. Each of you has left a lasting impact, not only on my game but on the way I approach challenges in life. Your lessons will stay with me far beyond the tennis court.

1. Mastering the Game: Life Skills on and off the Court

In the dynamic world of tennis, where every serve and volley is a testament to physical prowess and technical finesse, there exists a realm beyond the baseline—a space where life skills take center stage. Beyond the precision of strokes and the intensity of rallies, tennis becomes a stage for holistic development, where athletes cultivate not only their athletic prowess but also a reservoir of life skills that transcend the confines of the court. These skills become the backbone of a comprehensive sporting journey, shaping character, fostering emotional resilience, and paving the way for success within and beyond the tennis arena.

Life skills, as defined by the World Health Organization (WHO), are abilities that enable individuals to deal effectively with the demands and challenges of everyday life. In the context of sports like tennis, these skills go beyond the technical and tactical aspects of the game. They encompass a range of competencies that contribute to an athlete's mental and emotional development, helping them navigate both the pressures of competition and the broader challenges of life. Life skills include self-awareness, empathy, critical thinking, effective communication, interpersonal skills, decision-making, problem-solving, creative thinking, stress management, and coping with emotions.

The WHO recognizes the profound impact of life skills in sports, seamlessly integrating them into the very fabric of tennis. From the baseline to the net, the game transforms into a holistic and enriching experience, where these essential skills are the secret ingredients that elevate an athlete's performance and define their character both on and off the court. Tennis, with its unique blend of strategy, precision, and mental fortitude, becomes more than just a sport—it becomes a canvas for applying and refining these life skills, offering players a powerful toolkit for success in all areas of life.

As we explore life skills in the world of tennis, we'll uncover the intricate connections between these skills and the path to athletic success. Tennis serves as a microcosm of life, where each match is not just a test of physical abilities but also a crucible for developing resilience, leadership, and emotional intelligence. The discipline required to excel in tennis mirrors the discipline needed to navigate life's challenges, making the sport an ideal environment for fostering these essential life skills.

In the following chapters, each life skill will be carefully examined, its practical applications within the context of tennis explored, and its impact on every facet of an athlete's life revealed. Through illuminating interviews with coaches, athletes, and experts, we aim to shed light on how these skills not only shape athletic careers but also contribute immeasurably to the comprehensive development of individuals in the highly competitive and enriching world of sports.

From the baseline to the net, these chapters will unveil the specific applications of life skills within the sport, illustrating how they contribute to victories on the scoreboard and the victories of character and resilience that define a true tennis champion. As we unlock the potential of each life skill, it becomes evident that tennis transcends being just a game—it becomes a powerful avenue for acquiring skills that are ace in both sports and life.

"Tennis uses the language of life. Advantage, service, fault, break, love - The basic elements of tennis are those of everyday existence because every match is a life in miniature."

2. self-awareness

"I think self-awareness is probably the most important thing towards being a champion."

-   Billie Jean king

Self-awareness is a foundational life skill recognised by the World Health Organization (WHO) as essential for fostering holistic well-being, personal development, and effective functioning in both personal and professional spheres. At its core, self-awareness involves a deep, introspective understanding of one's inner landscape—encompassing thoughts, emotions, behaviours, strengths, weaknesses, and overall identity. This critical skill is a gateway to personal empowerment, enabling individuals to perceive themselves more clearly and accurately.

The journey to self-awareness begins with introspection, a process that encourages individuals to turn their attention inward and examine their internal states and reactions. This introspective process is not merely a passive reflection but an active exploration of the self to uncover the underlying motivations, beliefs, and values that drive behaviour. Through this exploration, individuals gain insight into the patterns that govern their thoughts and actions, allowing them to identify areas of strength and potential for growth.

One key benefit of self-awareness is its ability to foster emotional intelligence. By understanding and recognizing their emotions, individuals can better manage their emotional responses, leading to more balanced and thoughtful reactions in various situations. This emotional regulation is essential in high-pressure environments, such as sports or professional settings, where the ability to stay calm and composed can significantly impact performance and outcomes.

Moreover, self-awareness contributes to a more authentic and aligned life. When individuals clearly understand their values and aspirations, they are better equipped to make conscious choices that resonate with their true selves. This alignment between one's actions and inner values leads to a greater sense of fulfilment and purpose as individuals navigate their lives in a way consistent with their core beliefs.

In addition to personal growth, self-awareness also plays a crucial role in interpersonal relationships. By understanding their emotions and behaviours, individuals can communicate more effectively with others, fostering deeper connections and meaningful interactions. Self-aware individuals are more likely to approach relationships with empathy and understanding, recognizing the impact of their actions on others and striving to create positive, collaborative environments.

Self-awareness is an invaluable asset in leadership and teamwork. Self-aware leaders are better able to recognize their strengths and limitations, allowing them to lead with humility and confidence. They are also more attuned to the needs and emotions of their team members, fostering a supportive and inclusive environment that encourages collaboration and innovation. In this way, self-awareness enhances personal development and contributes to the success and cohesion of the groups and organizations to which individuals belong.

Furthermore, self-awareness is a diligent, ongoing process that evolves over time. It requires continuous learning and self-reflection as individuals navigate new experiences and challenges. By regularly engaging in mindfulness, journaling, and seeking feedback from others, individuals can deepen their self-awareness, gaining new insights and perspectives that enhance their personal and professional lives.

Self-awareness is more than just a life skill; it is a pathway to greater self-empowerment and fulfilment. Individuals can make informed decisions, build stronger relationships, and lead more purposeful lives by cultivating a deep and accurate understanding of themselves. In a world where external demands and expectations constantly change, self-awareness is a stable foundation, guiding individuals toward a life that aligns with their values, aspirations, and
authentic selves.

The Significance of self-awareness in Tennis:

Self-awareness plays a pivotal role in a tennis player's journey, guiding them through the multidimensional terrain of the court and providing profound insights into their strengths, weaknesses, and the intricate nuances of their game. Its significance extends beyond physical prowess, encompassing the mental and emotional dimensions that profoundly influence a player's performance. Let's explore the profound impact of self-awareness in the context of tennis:

Understanding Your Strengths and Weaknesses

Self-awareness is the foundation upon which a player's understanding of their strengths and weaknesses is built. It allows players to intimately know the areas where they excel and those where they need improvement. This insight is crucial for making strategic decisions on the court. Players can confidently approach each point by recognizing their strengths, whether it's a powerful serve, agile footwork, or precise shot placement. This self-assuredness translates into a more impactful game, where every move is executed purposefully.

Boosting Confidence

Armed with the knowledge of their strengths, self-awareness becomes a source of unshakable confidence. This confidence radiates in every aspect of a player's performance, from serving to moving across the court to the precision of shots. It's this self-belief that allows players to remain composed under pressure, turning the tide in their favour during critical moments of a match. The power of self-awareness lies in its ability to reinforce inner strength, enabling players to face any opponent with a heightened sense of assurance and poise.

Strategic Decision-Making

In tennis, every point is a battle of wits as much as it is of physical skill. When players are self-aware, they are equipped to make strategic decisions that play to their strengths. Knowing when to unleash a powerful serve, when to rely on agility, or when to place a shot with pinpoint accuracy becomes almost intuitive. Their game plan becomes more calculated, more effective, and more tailored to their unique style of play. This strategic edge, born from self-awareness, can be the difference between winning and losing a crucial point—or an entire match.

Letting Go of Perfection

One of the most liberating aspects of self-awareness is the realization that perfection is an unattainable goal in tennis. This understanding fosters a healthier mindset, where players can acknowledge areas for improvement without succumbing to the pressure of achieving flawless performance. Instead of striving for an impossible ideal, they learn to embrace imperfections as part of the game. This realistic perspective not only reduces unnecessary stress but also allows players to focus on continuous improvement rather than an elusive quest for perfection.

Discovering Your Unique Style

In the world of tennis, self-awareness is akin to discovering a player's unique playing style. It's about knowing what makes them stand out on the court—killer serves, quick footwork, or relentless endurance. Self-awareness acts as a personal touch-up tool by understanding their strengths and recognizing areas that need refinement, helping players craft a distinct style. This individuality sets them apart from other players and enhances their overall performance, making their style practical and memorable.

Choosing Wisely in the Heat of the Game

Tennis is a game of quick decisions where every moment counts. Self-awareness sharpens a player's ability to make wise choices under pressure based on a deep understanding of their tendencies and emotional triggers. They become acutely aware of how they react to high-stakes situations, their instinctively-made decisions, and the emotions that surface in critical moments. Armed with this knowledge, they can make informed, strategic decisions that align with their strengths and keep them calm and focused during crucial points in a match.

Setting Meaningful and Achievable Goals

Self-awareness plays a pivotal role in setting goals that resonate with a player's personal journey in tennis. It goes beyond merely understanding why they play the sport; it's about grasping why achieving specific goals holds personal significance for them. This connection transforms aspirations into ambitious yet realistic milestones. As a result, players feel a more profound sense of excitement and accomplishment with every step forward, whether refining particular aspects of their game, aiming for a specific ranking, or mastering advanced techniques. In this sense, self-awareness becomes the compass guiding a player's tennis journey with purpose and fulfilment.

Staying Cool Under Pressure

Tennis isn't just about hitting the ball; it's also about managing emotions and maintaining composure under pressure. Self-awareness is critical to recognizing and controlling emotional responses, whether dealing with a mistake's frustration or a high-stakes match's stress. By being self-aware, players can better understand their emotions and develop strategies to stay calm and composed, essential for performing at their best when the pressure is on.

Personal learnings

It took countless matches, many of which ended in disappointing losses, before I truly understood the power of self-awareness in tennis. I used to dwell on my mistakes, letting frustration and self-doubt take over, often leading to a downward spiral in my performance. During one particularly tough tournament, I found myself down a set, with my confidence shattered by a series of unforced errors. As I sat down during the changeover, the weight of previous losses and my tendency to fixate on mistakes loomed over me. It was then that something clicked—I realized that my biggest opponent wasn't the player across the net but my own mind.

I began to recognize the patterns that had been holding me back. I noticed how my focus would shift from playing my game to obsessing over what went wrong, trapping me in a cycle of negative thinking. At that moment, self-awareness kicked in. Instead of dwelling on the score or my past errors, I decided to acknowledge my frustration, let it go, and remind myself of my strengths: my serve, my footwork, and my ability to stay calm under pressure.

This wasn't an overnight change, but a gradual process developed over many matches where I learned to pause, reflect, and reset during the game. With this renewed mindset, I approached the next point with clarity and purpose, focusing on the present moment rather than the mistakes of the past. I started using my emotions as a guide, allowing them to inform my strategy rather than derail it. In that tournament match, this shift in focus allowed me to turn the game around, ultimately leading to victory.

This experience taught me that self-awareness isn't just about knowing your game—it's about recognising when your mind is working against you and having the presence of mind to refocus and play to your strengths. Over time, this shift in mindset has transformed how I play and how I view each challenge on the court, turning every match into an opportunity for growth rather than just a contest of skill.

At a crucial juncture in a tournament, I was down a set, with my confidence shaken by a series of unforced errors. Frustration was creeping in, clouding my judgment and throwing off my game. During the changeover, I took a moment to reflect—not on the score but on my mindset. I realised that my focus had shifted from playing my game to obsessing over mistakes. In that instant, self-awareness kicked in. I acknowledged my frustration, let it go, and reminded myself of my strengths: my serve and my ability to stay calm under pressure. With a fresh mindset, I approached the next point with clarity and purpose, turning the match around and ultimately winning; though that match was just another semi-finals, winning that match solidified my belief in the significance of self-awareness.

Building self-awareness on the Tennis Court:

Now, how do you cultivate this invaluable skill? Beyond being a game of forehands and backhands, tennis is a school of self-discovery. Here are some ways to build self-awareness through your tennis journey:

1. Regularly ask three key questions:

a.   What am I thinking?

Reflective Practice: Regularly pause and reflect on your thoughts during practice and matches. Understanding the patterns of your thoughts can unveil mental strategies that enhance focus or reveal areas needing adjustment.

b. How am I feeling?

Emotional Check-ins: Engage in emotional check-ins before and after training sessions. By acknowledging and articulating your emotions, you can develop a deeper understanding of how emotional states influence your performance.

c. How are my thoughts and feelings affecting my performance?

Performance Analysis: While reflecting or analysing your performance, notice the correlation between your thoughts, emotions, and on-court outcomes. This reflective analysis can unveil connections between mindset and performance, paving the way for targeted improvement.

2. Reflection

Consider keeping a tennis journal. Jot down your thoughts and feelings before, during, and after matches. It's a personal dialogue with yourself, revealing insights into your mental game. If conversations seem to be your interest, Engage in open conversations with your coach, peers, or even opponents. External feedback offers fresh perspectives, helping you see aspects of your game that might be in your blind spot.

3. Goal setting

Set goals that go beyond the scoreboard. Understand why you play tennis and what you aspire to achieve. Goals aligned with your values become guiding stars, steering you toward personal victories.

In tennis, self-awareness serves as your essential companion, guiding you to play your best game and enriching your journey both on and off the court. It functions like a trusted tennis buddy, helping you to cultivate resilience, focus, and confidence. With heightened self-awareness, you develop the mental tools necessary to navigate the challenges and celebrate the triumphs inherent in the sport.

While this discussion is contextualised within the realm of tennis, the principles of self-awareness are not limited to just this sport. These insights are equally applicable to any hobby or personal pursuit. Whether you're engaged in a different sport, involved in a cultural activity, or passionate about a personal interest, the benefits of self-awareness can enhance your experience and performance across various contexts. This book aims to show how these skills can be leveraged to improve not only your game but also your overall approach to any endeavour you undertake.

3. Empathy

"Your character is more important than how good you are at the sport. Your athleticism is only temporary, but your character, the type of person you are, lasts forever. be compassionate, be grateful, be honest, be humble."

-   Unknown.

Empathy, often described as the ability to understand and share the feelings of others, is much more than a mere act of sympathy; it is a profound life skill that serves as the cornerstone of meaningful human connections and personal development. According to the World Health Organization (WHO), empathy is a fundamental aspect of emotional intelligence and social growth. It encompasses the ability to not only recognize and acknowledge the emotions of those around us but also to deeply resonate with and respond to them in a way that fosters genuine understanding and connection.

Unlike sympathy, which involves a detached sense of pity or concern, empathy requires us to step into another person's shoes and experience their emotions from their perspective. This deeper level of engagement allows us to connect with others on a more personal and impactful level. It's about more than just recognizing someone's feelings; it's about feeling those emotions ourselves and responding in a way that truly supports and validates their experience.

Empathy is a dynamic and multi-dimensional skill that contributes to both personal growth and the enrichment of our relationships. It helps us build stronger, more resilient bonds with others by encouraging open communication, fostering trust, and creating a supportive environment where people feel valued and understood. By practicing empathy, we not only enhance our ability to navigate complex social interactions but also gain insight into our own emotional responses, leading to greater self-awareness and emotional maturity.

In essence, empathy is a vital component of emotional intelligence that enables us to connect with others on a profound level. It enriches our personal and professional relationships, promotes a deeper understanding of ourselves and those around us, and fosters an environment of mutual respect and support. As we develop our capacity for empathy, we pave the way for more meaningful interactions, personal growth, and a greater sense of compassion in our daily lives.

The Significance of Empathy in Tennis:

In the fast-paced and fiercely competitive world of tennis, the concept of empathy may seem like an abstract idea, overshadowed by the intensity of the game. Yet, empathy, often viewed as a cornerstone of effective interpersonal relationships, holds a profound significance in shaping the tennis experience for players, coaches, and fans alike. Far from being a mere supplementary trait, empathy is a powerful force that weaves understanding, respect, and collaboration into the fabric of the sport. Let's explore the multifaceted dimensions of empathy in tennis and uncover how this seemingly simple quality can transform the game.

In tennis, every match is more than just a contest of skills; it's a shared journey between competitors. Empathy bridges the gap between rivals, turning what could be a purely adversarial encounter into a collaborative experience. By recognizing and appreciating your opponent's dedication and passion, you create a unique connection that fosters mutual respect. This respect transcends mere recognition of skill; it involves a deep appreciation for each player's effort and sacrifices. Such understanding not only elevates the quality of the match but also enriches the experience for both players, turning competition into a meaningful exchange.

Empathy is equally crucial in team dynamics, particularly in doubles or team play. Here, understanding your teammate's struggles and celebrating their victories is essential for building a cohesive unit. Empathetic interactions transform individuals into a united force, where each player is attuned to the needs and emotions of their partners. This sense of unity goes beyond strategic coordination; it fosters a supportive environment where each member feels valued and understood. The result is a more harmonious and effective team, driven by a shared purpose and collective strength.

Communication is another area where empathy plays a vital role. Coaches who grasp their players' unique strengths and challenges empathetically are better equipped to create a winning formula. Empathetic communication leads to better coordination and smarter gameplay, as it establishes a playing environment where every player feels truly heard and supported. This understanding allows for more nuanced strategies and adjustments, enhancing overall performance on the court.

Tennis is often an emotional rollercoaster, filled with dramatic highs and lows. Empathy acts as a stabilizer, helping players navigate these emotional fluctuations with grace and resilience. Whether celebrating a hard-earned point or supporting an opponent facing a tough match, empathy creates an environment where emotions are acknowledged and managed constructively. This mutual support helps players handle the pressures of the game more effectively, fostering a sense of camaraderie even amidst fierce competition.

Respect, the heartbeat of tennis, is nurtured through empathy. Empathy lays the foundation for gracious winners and resilient individuals in the face of defeat by fostering an environment where players appreciate each other's efforts and challenges. It embodies the essence of sportsmanship, ensuring respect is maintained on and off the court. This respect is not limited to interactions between competitors but extends to the broader tennis community, enriching the sport as a whole.

In essence, empathy in tennis transcends the physicality of strokes and serves. It transforms the game into a shared experience of understanding and unity. Through empathy, tennis becomes not just a sport of competition but a journey of mutual respect and emotional connection. This quality enriches every aspect of the game, from personal interactions to team dynamics, and fosters an environment where every participant can thrive and grow.

Personal learning
My understanding of empathy was profoundly shaped by a couple of key experiences on the tennis court. During a particularly challenging match, I faced an opponent who had recently injured their ankle. Despite my initial focus on winning, I couldn't ignore their visible pain and frustration. This situation reminded me of a time when I had dealt with a similar injury and felt vulnerable and disheartened. Rather than

capitalizing on their predicament, I chose to offer encouragement and adjusted the pace of the game to help them manage their discomfort.

Another moment that deepened my appreciation for empathy occurred when my opponent's racket strings broke mid-match. Seeing their frustration, I immediately offered them one of my spare rackets. This gesture not only helped them continue the match but also fostered a spirit of camaraderie and mutual respect. These experiences taught me that empathy is about genuinely connecting with another's struggles and responding with care and support, which not only enhances sportsmanship but also builds meaningful connections both on and off the court.

Building Empathy on the Tennis Court

In the world of tennis, empathy is a powerful force that enhances not only individual performance but also the overall experience on and off the court. It starts with acknowledging your opponent's efforts recognizing the dedication and hard work they bring to the game. By appreciating their skills and passion for tennis, you foster a mutual respect and a shared love for the sport that transcends mere competition. This foundational respect also extends to teammates, transforming them from competitors to allies. In doubles or team play, understanding their struggles, celebrating their victories, and offering support during challenging moments builds a sense of unity and collaboration.

Beyond the perfect shot or the flawless serve, empathy serves as the true catalyst that transforms tennis from a mere sport into a celebration of human connections and shared experiences on the court. It infuses the game with depth and richness, making each match not just a test of skill but a meaningful interaction. By cultivating empathy, you elevate the game, turning every rally and exchange into an opportunity to build connections, foster mutual respect, and enrich the overall experience. Here's how you can weave empathy into the fabric of your tennis game and make it truly transformative:

1.Effective communication

Effective communication is a critical aspect of empathy in tennis. Both coaches and players benefit from empathetic interactions, which lead to better strategies and compelling gameplay. Active listening is essential— pay attention to each other's insights and experiences on the court, provide constructive feedback, and encourage an open exchange of ideas. Understanding individual playing styles, strengths, preferences, and areas for improvement allows you to tailor strategies that enhance each other's game. Constructive feedback should be seen as a roadmap for development, focusing on progress rather than perfection. A culture of open dialogue ensures that everyone feels heard and valued, creating a collaborative and engaging tennis journey.

2. Cultivate Respect On and Off the Court:

Foster an environment where respect is paramount, regardless of wins or losses. Encourage sportsmanship, display grace when you win, and resilience in defeat all underlined by a foundation of understanding and empathy. Here are some ways you can cultivate respect on the court:

Encourage Positive Body Language: Use positive body language, such as shaking hands, acknowledging the opponent's good shots, and maintaining composure during challenging moments.

Promote Fair Play: Engage in fair play at all times and adhere to rules. Call out your own faults and demonstrate honesty on the court.

Acknowledge Opponents: After a match, acknowledge and appreciate your opponent's efforts. It may be a handshake, a brief exchange of words, or a nod of respect.

Celebrate Good Shots: Celebrate not only your own successes but also applaud good shots made by your opponent. Doing this fosters a positive and supportive atmosphere.

Emphasize Learning from Each Match: Shift the focus from winning or losing to the lessons learned from each match. Discuss strategies, techniques, and areas for improvement rather than dwelling solely on the outcome.

Create a Team Environment: For doubles or team matches, foster a sense of camaraderie. Encourage and support each other, communicate effectively, and work together towards common goals.

Address Conflict Promptly: If conflicts arise, address them promptly and constructively. Discuss issues openly, find common ground, and work towards resolutions that benefit the team's dynamics.

3. Treat teammates and competitors as allies
Tennis brings together a diverse community, and embracing this diversity is critical to enriching the tennis experience. Appreciate the differences in playing styles, backgrounds, and

experiences, using them as opportunities to learn and grow. Support opponents through their challenges, fostering an atmosphere of sportsmanship. Finally, view every match as a learning experience, not just for yourself but also for your opponents and teammates. Embrace tennis lessons and share insights to grow as players and individuals collectively.

empathy in tennis is more than a mere courtesy—it is a transformative force that enriches the game by fostering genuine connections, mutual respect, and a supportive environment. By acknowledging and valuing the efforts of opponents, celebrating each other's successes, and navigating the emotional landscape of the game with compassion, you elevate tennis from a competitive sport to a profound human experience. Empathy allows players to build stronger relationships, enhance their own performance, and contribute to a more positive and inclusive atmosphere on the court.

The lessons of empathy explored in this chapter, while contextualized within the realm of tennis, hold universal relevance. The principles of understanding, respect, and support are not confined to the tennis court but extend to any sport, cultural event, or personal interaction. By applying these insights broadly, you can transform various aspects of life, fostering deeper connections and creating more fulfilling experiences in all areas of your journey.

4. Critical thinking

"Just believe yourself. Even if you dont, pretend that you do and, at some point, you will."
                                                            - Venus Williams

In an era where we are constantly bombarded with an avalanche of information and faced with a myriad of decisions daily, the ability to think critically stands out as an indispensable life skill. Critical thinking is not just a buzzword, but a crucial capability recognized by the World Health Organization (WHO) for its profound impact on navigating the intricate landscape of modern life. It empowers individuals to analyze information, evaluate evidence, and make well-reasoned decisions amidst the noise of conflicting data and opinions.

This chapter will embark on an exploration of the multifaceted nature of critical thinking, delving into its fundamental principles and illustrating its pivotal role in personal and professional spheres. We will unravel how critical thinking extends beyond mere problem-solving to become a strategic tool that shapes our approach to challenges, decision-making, and everyday interactions.

Moreover, we will shine a spotlight on the surprising ways in which engaging in sports, particularly tennis, can serve as a powerful catalyst for honing critical thinking skills. Tennis, with its dynamic blend of strategy, quick decision-making, and adaptability, offers a unique arena where critical thinking is not just encouraged but actively developed. By navigating the fast-paced scenarios on the court, players are continually refining their ability to assess situations, anticipate opponents' moves, and devise tactical responses.

Through insightful examples, personal anecdotes, and practical applications, this chapter will demonstrate how the principles of critical thinking are intricately woven into the fabric of sports. We will explore how the mental challenges faced in tennis mirror those encountered in broader contexts, reinforcing the idea that critical thinking is a versatile skill with far-reaching implications. So, prepare to dive into the world of critical thinking, discover its importance, and see how the lessons learned on the court can be applied to enhance decision-making and problem-solving in every facet of life.

The Significance of Critical Thinking in Tennis:

In the ever-evolving world of tennis, where every serve, volley, and rally demands not only physical prowess but also sharp mental acuity, critical thinking emerges as an indispensable asset. Critical thinking is vital to an athlete's success, exploring its multifaceted role in elevating a player's performance and strategic approach on the court.

Critical thinking in tennis transcends mere reactionary play; it involves a sophisticated blend of analysis, evaluation, and strategic decision-making. It is akin to solving an intricate puzzle where every move and countermove requires thoughtful consideration and adaptability. As players navigate the complexities of each match, critical thinking allows them to unravel their opponents' strategies, assess shifting conditions, and refine their own approach to achieve success.

The process begins with analysing opponents' strategies. On the court, understanding the nuances of your opponent's playstyle is crucial. It's not just about reacting to their moves but anticipating them. This analytical approach involves observing their strengths, recognizing their weaknesses, and predicting their next moves. By piecing together these insights, you position yourself to counter effectively, making informed decisions that keep you one step ahead. This strategic foresight transforms every match into a dynamic learning experience, continually evolving as you adapt and refine your game.

Evaluating on-court situations is another critical dimension. Tennis is a game of constant change, where variables such as ball speed, opponent movements, and surface conditions are in constant flux. Critical thinking equips players to assess these variables on the fly, enabling them to adjust their strategies precisely. Whether you are facing a powerful serve or dealing with an unexpected shift in play, the ability to evaluate and adapt your responses is crucial. This skill ensures that you remain agile, making split-second decisions that can alter the course of the game and capitalize on emerging opportunities.

Strategic decision-making is the heart-pounding core of every tennis match. Each encounter presents a unique set of challenges that demand a tailored approach. Critical thinking compels you to scrutinize the effectiveness of your strategies, identify areas for improvement, and refine your game plan. This ongoing evaluation process transforms every match into an opportunity for growth, where you approach each challenge with a mindset geared towards continuous learning and development.

The diverse playing conditions in tennis, from fast-paced grass courts to slow clay surfaces, further highlight the importance of critical thinking. Adapting to these varied environments requires a thoughtful approach. Embracing the challenge with curiosity and flexibility, critical thinkers relish the opportunity to adjust their game to suit the surface and conditions. This adaptability enhances performance and underscores the essential role of thinking in navigating the multifaceted nature of the sport.

Learning from defeats is another crucial aspect. Far from being mere setbacks, losses are valuable learning opportunities. Critical thinking enables you to dissect and analyze your defeats, extracting lessons that contribute to your growth as a player. By reflecting on what went wrong and identifying areas for improvement, you develop resilience and a deeper understanding of the game, preparing you for future challenges with renewed strength.

Ultimately, a continuous improvement mindset is fostered by critical thinking. This mindset acknowledges that the journey in tennis is as significant as the destination. Critical thinkers are open to seeking out new challenges, learning from every experience, and elevating their game to new heights. This commitment to perpetual growth propels players forward, ensuring they remain at the forefront of excellence on the court.

Critical thinking in tennis is transformative. It turns challenges into opportunities for growth, drives players to continually evolve, and propels them toward achieving new levels of excellence. By integrating critical thinking into your approach, you not only enhance your performance but also enrich your overall tennis experience.

Building Critical Thinking on the Tennis Court

Critical thinking is an invaluable skill, but at its core lies a fundamental ability: analysis. To truly excel in critical thinking, one must master the art of connecting logical ideas with real-world situations to gain a comprehensive understanding of the bigger picture. In the context of tennis, developing this skill involves a multifaceted approach, integrating various aspects of the game to enhance performance and strategy.

At its essence, critical thinking in tennis revolves around analyzing the myriad elements that influence a match. Begin by examining the court conditions. Different surfaces—be it grass, clay, or hard court—affect ball behavior and player movement in distinct ways. By understanding these nuances, you can adjust your game strategy to align with the specific demands of the surface. This kind of analysis helps you anticipate how the ball will bounce, how it will interact with the court, and how you can leverage these factors to your advantage.

Next, focus on analyzing your opponent's strengths and weaknesses. Every player has unique tendencies, from preferred shots to particular strategies they rely on. By observing and dissecting these tendencies, you can identify patterns that inform your game plan. For instance, if you notice that your opponent struggles with high topspin shots, you can incorporate more of these into your play to exploit this vulnerability. This kind of tactical analysis allows you to anticipate your opponent's moves and adapt your strategy accordingly.

Evaluating your strategies in real-time is another crucial component of building critical thinking. During a match, conditions and scenarios are constantly evolving. Critical thinking enables you to assess your current strategy, recognize when it's no longer effective, and make necessary adjustments. This could involve shifting your positioning, altering your shot selection, or changing your overall approach based on how the match unfolds.

The practice of analysis should not be limited to match play alone. To build critical thinking skills, integrate analytical exercises into your training routine. Analyze your performance during practice sessions, review match footage, and engage in mental simulations to refine your strategic thinking. By making analysis a regular part of your training, you enhance your ability to think critically in high-pressure situations, making these skills second nature.

Ultimately, the key to building critical thinking is consistent practice and application of analysis. By embedding analytical skills into your daily training regimen, you create a foundation upon which your critical thinking abilities can grow. This approach not only improves your game but also sharpens your overall strategic insight.

Reflecting on my own journey, I remember a match where my critical thinking skills were put to the test. Facing a formidable opponent known for his powerful serves and aggressive play, I initially struggled to keep up. However, by closely analyzing his game patterns and adapting my strategy, I noticed that he had a tendency to overcommit on his forehand shots. I adjusted my positioning and began targeting his weaker backhand side, which shifted the momentum in my favor. This experience underscored the importance of critical thinking, demonstrating how analyzing patterns and adapting strategies can turn the tide of a match.

Critical thinking is a cornerstone of success on the tennis court. It empowers players to analyze situations, adapt to varying conditions, and approach challenges with a solution-oriented mindset. While this chapter has contextualized critical thinking within the realm of tennis, the principles discussed are universally applicable. Whether in sports, professional environments, or personal endeavours, thinking critically enhances decision-making, problem-solving, and overall effectiveness. Embrace these insights as tools for growth, not only in tennis but in every facet of life.

5. Creative thinking

"I have always considered tennis as a combat in an arena between two gladiators who have their racquets and their courage as their weapons."

-   Yannick Noah

Creative thinking is the spark that ignites innovation and the drive that pushes boundaries. It's the ability to generate new, imaginative ideas, solutions, and perspectives that can transform the ordinary into the extraordinary. This kind of thinking requires looking beyond conventional limits, seeing connections between seemingly unrelated concepts, and finding fresh approaches to challenges that might otherwise seem insurmountable. By embracing creative thinking, we open ourselves up to questioning long-held assumptions, exploring uncharted possibilities, and expressing our ideas in ways that are uniquely our own.

In the context of sports like tennis, creative thinking can be the difference between following the same routine and discovering a strategy that sets you apart. It's about daring to experiment with new techniques, adjusting your style of play to surprise your opponent, or even inventing a shot that's never been seen before. Creative thinking encourages you to break away from the norm and explore the full range of your potential, not just as an athlete but as a problem-solver and innovator.

In this chapter, we'll delve into the essence of creative thinking, exploring how it can be cultivated and applied both on and off the court. Through various examples and practical exercises, you'll learn how to tap into your creative potential, turning challenges into opportunities and transforming your approach to the game—and life—with a fresh, inventive perspective.

The Significance of Creative Thinking in Tennis:

In the fast-paced, high-stakes world of tennis, where every point can make or break a match, creative thinking exceeds the boundaries of established play. It transforms the sport into an art form, blending strategy with innovation and precision with unpredictability. Creative thinking in tennis is not merely about flashy moves or unnatural shots; it is a vital component of a player's arsenal, providing a special advantage in the competitive arena. As you navigate the intense rallies and strategic battles, creativity becomes the force that can elevate your game to extraordinary heights.

Unleashing Unpredictability
Creative thinking is a powerful tool that introduces unpredictability into your game. Tennis is often a game of anticipation, where opponents try to predict your next move based on patterns and tendencies. By incorporating creative strategies, you disrupt this predictability, catching your opponents off guard. This unpredictability can manifest in various forms—whether through unexpected shot selection, unconventional court positioning, or innovative spins and angles. It's about keeping your opponent guessing, never letting them settle into a rhythm. This element of surprise not only puts pressure on your opponent but also gives you the psychological edge, making you a more challenging and difficult player to beat.

Adapting to Varied Playing Styles
Tennis is a sport rich with diversity in playing styles. Each opponent brings a unique approach to the game, from aggressive baseliners to crafty serve-and-volley players. Creative thinking is essential in adapting to these varied styles. It allows you to quickly assess your opponent's strengths and weaknesses and develop a strategy that maximizes your advantages while exploiting their vulnerabilities. Whether you're adjusting to the power of a big hitter or the finesse of a strategic player, creativity enables you to be versatile and adaptable, ensuring that you can thrive against any opponent. It's about seeing beyond the obvious and finding new ways to challenge and overcome your opponent.

Crafting Unique Shot Selections
The art of shot-making is where creativity truly shines in tennis. The ability to craft unique and unexpected shots adds depth and complexity to your game. It's not just about showcasing skill; it's about expanding your tactical repertoire. Creative shot selection can involve a variety of techniques, from drop shots and lobs to angled volleys and topspin-heavy forehands. These shots become your secret weapons, designed to catch your opponent off guard and force them into uncomfortable positions. By thinking creatively, you transform each rally into a chess match, where every shot is a calculated move that puts you closer to winning that point.

Strategic Point Construction
Creative thinking is also the foundation of strategic point construction. Tennis matches are often won by those who can outthink their opponents, not just outplay them. You can manipulate the game's flow by utilising creative strategies, strategically positioning yourself to exploit open spaces and create opportunities for winning shots. This involves more than just hitting the ball; it's about understanding the court, anticipating your opponent's reactions, and constructing points with finesse. Creative point construction separates good players from great ones—it's the ability to see the game several moves ahead and execute a plan that leads to victory.

Innovation in Movement and Positioning
Movement and positioning on the court are crucial aspects of tennis, and creativity plays a significant role in these areas as well. Innovative movement can give you an advantage, whether it's by approaching the net unexpectedly or by using defensive tricks to turn the tide of a rally. Creative positioning allows you to dictate the game's pace, putting you in control of the court. It's not just about where you stand; it's about how you move, how you anticipate your opponent's shots, and how you position yourself to capitalize on every opportunity. This creativity in movement and positioning is what makes your game more effective and your presence on the court more commanding.

Enhancing the Spectacle of the Sport
Finally, creative thinking doesn't just benefit you as a player; it enhances the overall spectacle of tennis. The sport is as much about entertainment as it is about competition, and creative play adds to its charm.

Unconventional shots, strategic surprises, and innovative plays contribute to the excitement and unpredictability that viewers love. By embracing creative thinking, you elevate tennis beyond a mere contest of skill, turning it into a captivating blend of athleticism and artistry. It's about making the game not just a competition but a celebration of creativity, where each match is an opportunity to showcase the beauty and brilliance of the sport.

In essence, creative thinking in tennis is about pushing the boundaries of what's possible, challenging the status quo, and finding new ways to succeed. It's a skill that enhances every aspect of your game, from strategy and shot selection to movement and mindset. By cultivating creativity on the court, you not only become a better player but also contribute to the evolution of the sport, making it more affluent, more engaged, and more exciting for everyone involved.

Building Creative Thinking on the Tennis Court

Creativity in tennis isn't just about making flashy shots or pulling off unexpected moves; it's about seeing the game through a different lens, where each stroke is an opportunity to explore, adapt, and express your unique style. Building creativity on the court starts with a mindset shift. It's about playing for the pure enjoyment of the game, allowing yourself the freedom to experiment without the fear of failure. When you step onto the court, think of it as a canvas, where every point is a brushstroke that adds to the larger picture of your tennis journey.

The journey of building creative thinking in tennis begins with curiosity. Start by exploring different shots and angles, even if they seem abnormal. For example, when practicing, try hitting the same shot with varying degrees of spin, pace, or placement. Notice how the ball reacts to different surfaces or weather conditions, and consider how you can use these factors to your advantage in a match. This kind of experimentation helps you develop a broader repertoire of skills that you can draw upon during competition. It's like learning a new language—each shot is a new word, and the more words you know, the more expressive you can be.

Another way to cultivate creativity is through observation. Watch other players, not just the professionals but also your peers. Notice how they construct points, how they adapt to different opponents, and how they handle pressure. Then, incorporate what you learn into your own game. For instance, if you observe a player who excels at drop shots, practice this shot until it becomes a natural part of your game. By blending your observations with your own instincts, you begin to create a style that is both effective and uniquely yours.

Adapting to various playing styles is another crucial aspect of building creativity. Tennis is a sport where you often encounter opponents with vastly different approaches to the game. Some may rely on powerful serves, while others might focus on consistent baseline play. Instead of sticking rigidly to your usual tactics, creative thinking encourages you to adapt. Maybe you experiment with coming to the net more often against a baseline player or use a variety of spins to disrupt an opponent's rhythm. This adaptability not only makes you a more versatile player but also keeps your opponents on their toes, unsure of what to expect next.

Creativity also thrives in the face of challenges. During a tough match, when your usual strategies aren't working, creative thinking is what allows you to pivot. Perhaps the wind is affecting your serve, or your opponent has figured out your baseline game. Instead of sticking to what's not working, think outside the box. Maybe you start mixing in more drop shots or change your positioning on the court. Each challenge is an opportunity to innovate, to find a solution that might not be obvious but could turn the match in your favor.

Ultimately, building creativity in tennis is about playing with a sense of freedom and joy. When you allow yourself to enjoy the process, to take risks without fearing mistakes, your game naturally becomes more dynamic and expressive. Creativity is not just about finding new ways to win but also about enhancing your overall experience of the sport.

In conclusion, while this chapter focuses on building creative thinking in tennis, the lessons extend far beyond the court. Whether you're engaged in another sport, pursuing a hobby, or facing challenges in everyday life, the principles of creativity—exploration, observation, adaptation, and joyful experimentation—are universally applicable. By embracing creativity, you open yourself to new possibilities, not just in tennis but in every aspect of life.

Personal learning
During a particular match, I was up against my coach, an opponent who knew my game in and out, and was able to anticipate every move I made, every shot I hit. My usual strategies weren't working. Instead of sticking to my routine, I decided to try something different—mixing up my shots in ways I hadn't before. I began incorporating unexpected drop shots and varying the spin on my groundstrokes, pushing myself to think creatively on the fly. At one point, I even surprised myself by coming to the net more frequently, forcing my opponent to adjust to my new, unpredictable style. This shift in approach not only turned the match around but also taught me a valuable lesson: that creativity on the court isn't just about mastering new techniques—it's about having the confidence to experiment, adapt, and trust your instincts when the game demands it.

6. Decision making

"Freed from the thoughts of winning, I instantly play better. I stop thinking, start feeling. My shots become a half-second quicker, my decisions become the product of instinct rather than logic."

- Andre Agassi

Life unfolds as a series of decisions, each one shaping the path we take and influencing the person we become. From the simplest choices, like deciding what to wear or what to eat, to the life-altering decisions about our careers, relationships, and personal values, the ability to make informed and thoughtful decisions is a cornerstone of our growth and success. This decision-making process is not just about choosing between options; it's about weighing possibilities, understanding consequences, and ultimately steering our lives in a direction that aligns with our goals and aspirations.

The importance of decision-making cannot be overstated, and the World Health Organization (WHO) recognizes it as one of the essential life skills necessary for an individual's holistic development. Decision-making is intertwined with every aspect of our lives, influencing our mental, emotional, and physical well-being. It equips us to navigate the complexities of the modern world, where the pace of change is rapid, and the demands on our time and attention are relentless.

In this chapter, we delve into the significance of decision-making, examining how it is not only a skill but a discipline that can be cultivated and refined. Through the lens of sports, particularly tennis, we will explore how the practice of making quick, strategic decisions on the court can translate into better decision-making in everyday life. Tennis, with its rapid pace and constant need for strategy, serves as an excellent metaphor for the decision-making process in life. Every serve, every rally, and every point in a match is a decision that requires clarity, focus, and foresight.

The Significance of decision-making in Tennis:

In tennis, every match is a complex interplay of strategy, skill, and split-second decisions. The significance of decision-making in tennis cannot be overstated, as it is the very heart of the sport. Unlike many other sports where team dynamics play a significant role, tennis is an individual game, requiring players to rely solely on their own judgment to outmanoeuvre their opponents. This places immense pressure on a player's ability to make the right decisions under varying conditions, often with little time to think. It's not just about physical skill, but also about the mental understanding required to outsmart the opponent.

Each point in tennis is a microcosm of the decision-making process. From the moment the ball is served, a player must assess a multitude of factors—the opponent's position, the speed and spin of the ball, the conditions of the court, and their own physical and mental state. Within seconds, they must decide how to respond: whether to go for a powerful baseline shot, a delicate drop shot, or a risky passing shot down the line. The success of these decisions directly impacts the outcome of the match, making decision-making an indispensable aspect of the game.

What sets apart the good players from the great ones is their ability to consistently make the right decisions, especially under pressure. The margins in tennis are razor-thin; a single poorly judged shot can turn the tide of an entire match. Therefore, the significance of decision-making is amplified in high-stakes situations, such as breakpoints or match points, where the pressure is at its peak. Players who can maintain their composure and make sound decisions in these moments are often the ones who succeed.

Moreover, decision-making in tennis is not just about the immediate shot selection but also about long-term strategy. A match can last several hours, requiring players to think several steps ahead, anticipate their opponent's moves, and adjust their game plan accordingly. This strategic aspect of decision-making is what makes tennis not just a physical contest but a mental one as well. Players must constantly evaluate what is working and what isn't, making real-time adjustments to their tactics in order to exploit their opponent's weaknesses while minimizing their own vulnerabilities.

Decision-making in tennis also involves managing the psychological aspects of the game. Tennis is as much a mental battle as it is a physical one, with players needing to decide how to handle their emotions, whether it's staying calm after losing a crucial point or keeping their focus when they're on the brink of victory. The ability to manage one's mental state and make clear-headed decisions, even when the stakes are high, is a crucial determinant of a player's success.

Additionally, the significance of decision-making in tennis extends beyond the match itself. It plays a crucial role in a player's overall development and career trajectory. Choosing when to push for a win and when to play it safe, deciding which tournaments to enter, how to train, and how to recover from injuries—all these decisions shape a player's career. Successful tennis players are those who not only make the right decisions on the court but also off it, managing their careers with the same strategic mindset they bring to their matches.

Decision-making in tennis is the thread that weaves together the physical, mental, and strategic elements of the game. It is what allows players to navigate the complexities of the sport, turning challenges into opportunities and setbacks into opportunities. Whether in the heat of a match or in the broader context of their careers, the significance of decision-making in tennis cannot be underestimated. It is the skill that elevates the game from mere physical competition to a profound test of intellect, character, and resilience, making tennis one of the most mentally demanding and rewarding sports in the world.

Building decision-making skills on the Tennis Court

Building decision-making skills on the tennis court is a vital aspect of advancing your game. Tennis, unlike many other sports, places you in a position where every choice can dictate the direction of the match. Whether you're deciding how to approach a critical point or determining your overall strategy, the ability to make informed, confident decisions can be the difference between victory and defeat. Let's delve into the process of cultivating these skills on the court and how they can transform your performance.

Court Awareness
The foundation of effective decision-making in tennis begins with court awareness. This isn't just about knowing where the lines are or understanding the dimensions of the court—it's about developing a deep familiarity with the surface, the way the ball behaves on different terrains, and how your own game adjusts to these variables. For instance, playing on a clay court requires a different approach than playing on grass or hard court. The bounce of the ball, the speed of the surface, and even the weather conditions play a significant role in how you should respond. By honing your court awareness, you can anticipate these factors and make smarter decisions regarding your shot selection, positioning, and strategy.

Match Situation Evaluation
Decision-making in tennis is highly contextual. Understanding the current state of the match is crucial for making the right decisions. Are you ahead in the game, or are you trying to catch up? Is your opponent showing signs of fatigue, or are they gaining momentum? Evaluating the match situation involves constantly reassessing these variables and adjusting your strategy accordingly. For example, if you're leading in a set, it might be wise to play more conservatively, reducing unforced errors and maintaining your advantage. On the other hand, if you're trailing, you might need to take more calculated risks to shift the momentum in your favor. Developing this situational awareness allows you to make decisions that are aligned with your overall match strategy, ensuring that you're always playing with purpose and intent.

Opponent Analysis
Another critical aspect of decision-making in tennis is understanding
your opponent. Every player has their own strengths, weaknesses, and
tendencies. Some may have a powerful serve but struggle with their
backhand, while others might excel at the net but falter in long baseline
rallies. By analyzing your opponent's game, you can tailor your
decisions to exploit their vulnerabilities. This might mean targeting their
weaker side with consistent shots, forcing them into uncomfortable
positions, or varying your play to keep them off-balance. The ability to
read your opponent and adapt your strategy based on this analysis is what
separates good players from great ones.

Strategic Moves
Incorporating strategic moves into your game is essential for effective
decision-making. Tennis isn't just about hitting the ball back and forth;
it's about outthinking your opponent. Strategic moves such as when to
approach the net, when to play defensively, or when to go for a winner
are all decisions that can tip the balance of a match. For instance,
approaching the net can put pressure on your opponent, forcing them to
make quick decisions, while staying back might allow you to control the
rally from the baseline. Understanding when and how to use these
strategies is key to keeping your opponent guessing and maintaining
control of the match.

Risk Management
Tennis is a game of calculated risks. Every shot you make carries some
level of risk, whether it's the chance of hitting the ball out of bounds or
the opportunity it gives your opponent to counterattack. Effective
decision-making involves assessing these risks and making choices that
maximize your chances of success while minimizing potential
downsides. For example, going for a risky winner might be appropriate
when you're confident in your shot, but playing it safe might be better
when you're unsure or facing a crucial point. Balancing aggression with
caution is a delicate art, and mastering it can significantly improve your
overall performance.

Adaptability Exercises
Building decision-making skills also involves cultivating adaptability.
Tennis matches are dynamic, with conditions and circumstances
constantly changing. Whether it's the weather, the condition of the court,
or your opponent's evolving strategy, you need to be able to adjust on the
fly. This adaptability can be developed through specific drills and

exercises that simulate different match scenarios. For instance, practicing under varying weather conditions or against different types of opponents can help you build the resilience and flexibility needed to make smart decisions, no matter what the match throws at you.

Quick Decision Drills
Tennis often requires split-second decisions, where there's no time for second-guessing. Quick decision-making drills can help you sharpen your reflexes and improve your ability to make the right choices in real-time. These drills might involve rapid-fire shot selection, where you have to choose your shots quickly based on the ball's trajectory, or exercises that require you to decide on your next move within a strict time constraint. These practices simulate the fast pace of a real match, helping you develop the instinctive decision-making skills that are crucial for success on the court.

Personal Experience: Learning Decision-Making on the CourtThere was a crucial moment in my tennis career when a split-second decision during a match made all the difference. I was deep into a challenging match, and in the middle of a rally, I felt a sharp pain in my leg. I knew something wasn't right, but I was torn between pushing through the pain and playing it safe. My competitive spirit urged me to keep going, but I made the tough decision to retire from the match, fearing that continuing could worsen the injury. It was a hard pill to swallow—I lost that match, and it felt like a defeat at the time. However, that decision turned out to be one of the best I've ever made. By stepping back and allowing my leg to heal, I avoided a more severe injury. Just a few weeks later, fully recovered, I entered a much bigger tournament, playing some of the best tennis of my life and ultimately winning the title. That experience taught me that sometimes, the best decision isn't the one that wins the immediate battle, but the one that positions you to win the war.

While the context of this discussion has been tennis, the principles of decision-making are universally applicable. Whether in sports, academics, or daily life, the ability to make informed, strategic decisions is crucial for success. The skills developed on the tennis court—such as court awareness, situational evaluation, opponent analysis, and adaptability—are not just limited to the game; they translate into valuable life skills that can guide you through a variety of challenges. The practice of decision-making in tennis can serve as a powerful tool for personal growth, helping you navigate the complexities of life with confidence and clarity. Just as in tennis, where every decision matters, so too in life, each choice we make shapes our journey, determining our path to success.

7. Problem solving

"There's no way around hard work. Embrace it"

-   Roger Federer

In today's evolving world, the ability to solve problems effectively is not just a valuable skill but an essential one for navigating both personal and professional landscapes. Recognized by the World Health Organization (WHO) as a fundamental life skill, problem-solving surrounds more than finding answers to immediate issues. It involves a strategic approach to understanding, analyzing, and addressing challenges in a way that drives meaningful progress and success.

At its core, problem-solving is a multi-dimensional skill that integrates analytical thinking, creative insight, and resilience. It empowers individuals to break down complex issues into manageable components, consider various perspectives, and develop innovative solutions. This skill is crucial in a variety of contexts, from everyday life and career challenges to navigating interpersonal relationships and overcoming obstacles. Effective problem-solving enables people to transform difficulties into opportunities, making it a cornerstone of personal growth and professional achievement.

In the realm of tennis, problem-solving takes on a unique character. Tennis players are constantly presented with a series of unpredictable scenarios that require quick thinking and strategic planning. Whether it's adapting to an opponent's unexpected tactics, responding to changing court conditions, or managing the pressure of a high-stakes match, the sport demands a high level of problem-solving understanding. Tennis offers a live-action laboratory where players must continually assess and adjust their strategies in real-time. This not only hones their ability to think critically but also enhances their adaptability and decision-making skills.

This chapter will delve into how the sport of tennis exemplifies the art of problem-solving through its intricate challenges and fast-paced nature.

By exploring how players navigate the complexities of the game—such as analyzing opponents, adjusting strategies, and overcoming mental and physical hurdles—we will uncover valuable insights into the problem-solving process. We will also highlight how these lessons extend beyond the court, offering strategies and approaches that can be applied to various aspects of life. Through a detailed examination of problem-solving in tennis, we aim to provide a comprehensive understanding of this essential skill and its broader implications for personal and professional success.

The Significance of Problem-Solving in Tennis:

The significance of problem-solving in tennis is deep, extending well beyond the primary demands of the court and becoming a vital ingredient in a player's overall success. Tennis, with its kinetic pace and relentless demands, serves as a crucible where problem-solving skills are honed and tested under pressure. This skill is not merely about addressing immediate issues; it encompasses the ability to anticipate, adapt, and respond to countless challenges in real time.

Adapting to Opponents:
Tennis is a game of constant evolution, where each opponent introduces a new set of challenges and strategies. Problem-solving in this context means quickly analyzing an opponent's strengths and weaknesses and adjusting your game plan accordingly. For instance, if an opponent employs a powerful shot or has a clear stregnth, a player must swiftly devise a counter-strategy. This ability to adapt and recalibrate strategies on the fly is essential for gaining a competitive advantage and turning the rythem of a match in one's favour.

Strategic Shot Selection:
On the tennis court, each shot is a strategic decision, and problem-solving manifests in choosing the right shot at the right moment. Players must navigate a range of shot possibilities, from aggressive winners to defensive lobs, based on the context of the rally and the opponent's positioning. This split-second decision-making, influenced by the game's flow and court conditions, can dramatically impact the outcome of a point. The capacity to make these decisions under pressure highlights the crucial role of problem-solving in shaping the match

Handling match dynamics :
Every tennis match unfolds with its own unique rhythm, and problem-solving skills are essential for managing these dynamics. Players must continuously assess the match's evolving situation, including momentum shifts and score fluctuations. This requires a keen awareness of when to adjust tactics, whether it's tightening up play during a losing streak or capitalizing on a winning streak. The ability to navigate these fluctuations and maintain control over the game's momentum is a testament to effective problem-solving.

Overcoming Setbacks:
Tennis is as much a mental game as it is a physical one. When faced with setbacks, such as losing a set or falling behind in a game, problem-solving becomes a critical tool for recovery. Analyzing what went wrong, identifying areas for improvement, and devising a new strategy are essential steps for mounting a comeback. The mental resilience to address and overcome these challenges reflects the profound impact of problem-solving on a player's performance.

Adapting to Court Conditions:
The diversity of tennis surfaces—from the fast-paced hard courts to the slow, unpredictable clay—requires players to adapt their game strategies accordingly. Problem-solving involves understanding how each surface affects ball behavior and adjusting techniques to optimize performance. This adaptability not only enhances a player's versatility but also provides a strategic advantage by exploiting the specific characteristics of each surface.

Tactical Maneuvers:
Beyond individual shots, problem-solving extends to broader tactical decisions. Whether it's deciding when to approach the net, employ a drop shot, or adjust positioning, these decisions are pivotal in outmaneuvering opponents. Effective problem-solving in this regard involves evaluating the situation and making strategic choices that align with the overall game plan, thus gaining a tactical advantage.

Navigating High-Pressure Moments:
In critical moments, such as tiebreaks or match points, the pressure to perform is immense. Problem-solving in these scenarios involves staying composed and making sound decisions that can determine the match's outcome. The ability to think clearly and strategically under such pressure underscores the significance of problem-solving in high-stakes situations.

Building Problem-Solving skills on the Tennis Court

Analytical Awareness:
Begin by sharpening your observational skills. Every match is unique, and your first task is to analyze it piece by piece. Pay close attention to your opponent's playing style, their strengths, and their weaknesses. Is their serve predictable? Do they struggle with high balls? Understanding these elements allows you to formulate effective strategies and make adjustments in real time. This analytical awareness helps you anticipate your opponent's moves and prepare counter-strategies that could shift the momentum in your favour.

Adaptability Drills:
To thrive on the tennis court, you must be prepared for a variety of scenarios. Engage in drills that simulate changing game conditions, such as varying the pace, adjusting the court surface, or playing different opponents to experience various playing styles. By practicing under diverse conditions, you build the flexibility to adapt your tactics and shot selection based on the specific challenges you face. This fosters resilience, which is crucial for adjusting your game plan during a match.

Review and Reflect:
After each match or practice session, take the time to review your performance. Analyze instances where you faced challenges and assess the effectiveness of your problem-solving strategies. Reflect on what worked, what didn't, and why. This process of self-evaluation and learning from both successes and mistakes is crucial for continuous improvement. It allows you to refine your strategies and enhance your problem-solving skills over time.

Quick Decision Exercises:
Incorporate exercises that require rapid decision-making into your training routine. This could involve quick-fire shot selection drills or making strategic decisions within a limited timeframe. These exercises mirror the fast-paced nature of real matches and help you develop the ability to make quick, effective decisions under pressure.

Continuous Learning:
View each match as an opportunity to learn and grow. Embrace mistakes as valuable lessons and seek feedback from coaches or experienced players. This mindset of continuous learning helps you refine your problem-solving skills and adapt your strategies to evolving challenges. Always be open to new insights and approaches to enhance your game.

Off-Court Mental Training:
Enhance your cognitive abilities with off-court mental training. Activities such as puzzles, chess, or strategic games can sharpen your problem-solving skills and improve your overall mental acuity. By incorporating these activities into your routine, you build a strong foundation for effective problem-solving on the court.

Personal experiences of utilising Problem solving:
Balancing academics, extracurricular activities, and a demanding tennis schedule was one of the most challenging phases of my life, but it was through problem-solving that I found my way through. Juggling rigorous school work, competing in tournaments, and engaging in various extracurriculars required meticulous planning and adaptability. When faced with overlapping deadlines or unexpected changes, I used problem-solving skills to prioritize tasks, delegate responsibilities when possible, and adjust my strategies dynamically. For instance, when an important tournament coincided with crucial exam preparations, I devised a schedule that allocated focused time for both, ensuring that neither was compromised. By breaking down each challenge into manageable steps and seeking innovative solutions, I not only managed to excel in each area but also developed a resilience that has served me well beyond the court and classroom. This experience underscored the power of problem-solving as a universal tool for overcoming obstacles and achieving success in any aspect of life.

To conclude, The skills cultivated through tennis problem-solving are transferable to numerous aspects of life. In professional settings, the ability to analyze complex situations, make informed decisions, and adapt strategies is invaluable. Whether you're navigating a challenging project, addressing workplace conflicts, or making career decisions, the problem-solving skills developed on the tennis court provide a strong foundation for effective and strategic thinking.

In personal life, the problem-solving abilities refined through tennis can enhance your capacity to tackle daily challenges, manage relationships, and achieve personal goals. The resilience built through overcoming setbacks on the court translates to a greater ability to handle adversity and maintain a positive outlook in the face of difficulties.

Moreover, the practice of reviewing performance, embracing mistakes as learning opportunities, and continuously seeking improvement on the court mirrors the approach needed for growth in various life scenarios. Just as a tennis player reflects on their match to refine their strategies, individuals in all walks of life benefit from self-evaluation and a commitment to ongoing learning.

while the context of problem-solving discussed in this chapter is centered on tennis, its principles are universally relevant. The ability to analyze, adapt, and devise effective solutions is a milestone of success in any endeavor. By applying these problem-solving skills developed through the sport, you can enhance your capabilities and achieve excellence in both personal and professional realms. The journey on the tennis court is not just about mastering the game; it's about preparing for a lifetime of challenges and opportunities, equipped with the tools to solve problems and thrive in all aspects of life.

8. Effective communication

"Communication is the solvent of all problems and is the foundation for personal development."

- *Peter Shepherd*

Effective communication is the bedrock of meaningful human interaction and a fundamental life skill indispensable for navigating the complexities of modern life. At its essence, communication transcends mere exchange of words; it is about the artful conveyance of information, thoughts, and emotions with clarity and intention. This involves not only expressing oneself effectively through verbal means—such as choosing the right words and constructing coherent sentences—but also through nonverbal cues like body language, facial expressions, and tone of voice. The depth of effective communication also includes active listening, where one genuinely engages with and understands the speaker's message, acknowledging their perspective and responding thoughtfully.

Moreover, communication is deeply intertwined with empathy, the ability to perceive and resonate with the emotions and viewpoints of others, fostering a deeper connection and mutual understanding. This skill extends beyond individual interactions to encompass cultural and contextual sensitivity, ensuring that messages are appropriately adapted to diverse audiences and varying situations. In an increasingly interconnected world, where interactions span different cultures and contexts, the ability to navigate these nuances becomes even more critical.

Mastering effective communication is crucial for building and maintaining robust personal and professional relationships, resolving conflicts, and achieving success across various facets of life. Whether in fostering collaborative teamwork, advancing career goals, or managing personal relationships, the ability to communicate effectively can significantly influence outcomes and overall satisfaction. As we delve into this chapter, we will explore the principles and practices of effective communication, examining how these skills can be cultivated and applied to enhance interactions and drive success in our multifaceted world. Through practical examples and insights, we will uncover the transformative power of communication and its role in shaping our experiences and achievements.

The Significance of Effective Communication in Tennis:

Effective communication in tennis is a multifaceted skill that extends far beyond the court's physical boundaries. While the sport is often celebrated for its intense individual battles, the role of communication—both with oneself and with others—is crucial to achieving success and excelling in this demanding game.

At its core, communication in tennis involves conveying strategies, feedback, and support between players, coaches, and even opponents. For singles players, self-communication is vital. It encompasses the internal dialogue that helps players manage stress, focus on tactical adjustments, and maintain motivation. For example, a player might use positive self-talk to overcome moments of doubt or to reinforce their game plan during critical points in a match. This internal communication fosters mental resilience, helping players navigate the emotional highs and lows of competition.

In doubles tennis, the significance of communication is even more pronounced. Effective verbal and nonverbal exchanges between partners are essential for coordinating movements, executing strategies, and maintaining a cohesive game plan. Partners must communicate seamlessly to cover the court efficiently, decide on shot selections, and provide mutual encouragement. Clear, concise communication can prevent misunderstandings and errors, ensuring that both players are aligned in their approach and response to opponents' plays. For instance, pre-match discussions about strategies, signals during play, and post-match feedback are integral to building chemistry and optimizing performance.

Moreover, communication in tennis extends to interactions with opponents. Sportsmanship and respect are communicated through actions and words, setting a tone for fair play and a positive competitive environment. Effective communication can also help in resolving conflicts and maintaining a professional demeanor, which is essential for preserving the integrity of the sport.

Building Effective Communication skills on the Tennis Court

Body Language
In the realm of tennis, body language is a profound form of individual communication that transcends spoken words. It serves as a silent yet powerful means of conveying emotions, intentions, and states of mind, significantly influencing both personal performance and interactions with others.

On the tennis court, body language manifests in various ways: from the way a player stands before serving, to their reactions after a winning shot or a missed opportunity. A player's posture—whether it's a confident, upright stance or a slouched, defeated demeanour—communicates volumes about their mental state. For instance, an erect posture and assertive movements can signal confidence and readiness, while hunched shoulders and slow movements may convey frustration or fatigue. This non-verbal communication impacts not only how opponents perceive a player but also how they perceive themselves. A player who consciously adopts positive body language can bolster their own morale and project an image of composure, even when faced with adversity.

Good body language on the court extends beyond self-perception; it teaches players valuable lessons in how to communicate effectively in broader contexts. By becoming attuned to their own body language and its impact, players learn to be more mindful of how their non-verbal cues can influence interactions. This awareness translates into improved communication skills in everyday life. For example, being conscious of maintaining open, confident body language during conversations can help convey sincerity and approachability, enhancing personal and professional relationships.

Moreover, understanding and interpreting others' body language in tennis helps players develop a nuanced sense of non-verbal communication. Recognizing an opponent's subtle cues—such as a change in grip or posture—can provide insights into their strategy and emotional state. This ability to read and respond to body language can be transferred to real-life situations, where interpreting non-verbal signals can be crucial for effective communication and relationship-building.

Body language, not only help enhance the way an individual player communicates themselves to the audience and opponents, but also helps you effectively read your opponents to use it ultimately for your advantage.

Active Listening
Active listening is an important concept of effective communication on the tennis court. It involves hearing, understanding, and responding to input from your partner, coach, or team. Develop active listening skills by giving full attention to the speaker, whether they are providing instructions, feedback, or encouragement. Practice responding thoughtfully and making adjustments based on their input. By actively listening and responding to feedback, you enhance your ability to adapt and improve, ultimately leading to better performance on the court.

The principles of communication, though rooted in the context of tennis here, provide a framework that is adaptable to any situation. By integrating these communication strategies into everyday life, individuals can enhance their ability to connect with others, navigate challenges, and achieve their goals. Embracing and refining these skills not only leads to greater success on the tennis court but also cultivates a more fulfilling and harmonious existence across all facets of life.

These lessons in communication have broad applications in real life. In personal relationships, expressing oneself clearly and interpreting others' non-verbal cues can strengthen connections and resolve conflicts more amicably. In professional settings, effective communication enhances teamwork, aids in the negotiation process, and fosters a collaborative environment. These skills facilitate better interactions and enrich the overall experience for those engaged in other hobbies or interests.

Personal experience and learning
During one of my training sessions, my coach made it abundantly clear that body language was not just a matter of personal style but a critical component of performance. I was struggling with my game that day, and my frustration began to show through my body language—I slouched between points, grimaced with every mistake, and exuded an overall sense of defeat.

My coach, who was always keen on maintaining a positive and constructive atmosphere, took a firm stance. He stopped the session and pointedly addressed my lack of positive body language. With a stern approach, he explained that in tennis, as in life, projecting a positive and confident demeanour is essential not only for personal morale but also for maintaining the right mindset and composure under pressure. He then took the unusual step of asking me to leave the practice court until I could return with the right attitude.

At first, I was frustrated and confused by this decision, but as I reflected on it, I began to understand the deeper lesson. My coach wasn't simply concerned with my performance in that single practice; he was teaching me the vital role body language plays in communication and overall effectiveness on the court. By making me step away, he emphasized that positive body language wasn't just an option—it was a non-negotiable aspect of my training and competition.

This experience was a turning point for me. It taught me that body language significantly impacts how we are perceived and how effectively we communicate, even in an individual sport like tennis. I realized that how I present myself on the court can influence not only my own mental state but also the dynamics of a match and my interactions with coaches and opponents.

The lesson learned about the importance of maintaining positive body language during practice has since been a guiding principle in my approach to both tennis and life. It has underscored the idea that effective communication extends beyond words and includes the non-verbal cues we give off. This understanding has enhanced my ability to remain composed, confident, and engaging in various situations, proving that the principles of body language and communication are universally valuable.

9. Interpersonal relationships

"Effective teamwork begins and ends with communication"

\- *Mike Krzyzewski*

diam vel, facilisis quam. Vestibulum eget leo dui. Vestibulum mollis dui eu elit suscipit, quis ultrices eros cursus. Quisque nec purus tempor, vehicula dolor et, faucibus enim. Cras porta, est nec maximus finibus, risus lorem dignissim urna, lobortis euismod ipsum mauris imperdiet purus.

Interpersonal relationships, the cornerstone of human interaction, play a pivotal role in shaping our emotional and social experiences. These relationships, recognized by the World Health Organization (WHO) as a fundamental life skill, significantly influence our overall quality of life. They involve more than just establishing bonds; they encompass the art of maintaining meaningful connections through effective communication, empathy, and collaboration.

Building and nurturing these relationships require a deep understanding of both verbal and nonverbal communication, active listening, and the ability to navigate conflicts with grace and resilience. Effective communication enables individuals to express themselves clearly and understand others. However, it's empathy that truly fosters genuine connections by appreciating and valuing diverse perspectives. Active listening plays a crucial role in ensuring that interactions are respectful and that all parties feel heard and understood.

Conflict resolution and cooperation are equally essential, playing a significant role in managing disagreements constructively and working together towards common goals. Mastering these skills is not only crucial for emotional well-being but also for achieving social success and personal growth. Whether in personal relationships, professional settings, or casual interactions, the ability to connect with others meaningfully can profoundly impact our happiness, productivity, and overall life satisfaction.

In this chapter, we delve into the significance of interpersonal relationships and explore how developing these skills can enhance various aspects of our lives. Through an examination of effective communication strategies, empathetic interactions, and conflict management, we will uncover how these principles can be applied to build stronger, more fulfilling relationships, both in and out of the tennis court.

The Significance of Interpersonal relationships in Tennis:

The significance of interpersonal relationships in tennis extends far beyond the individual pursuit of excellence. In a sport often viewed through the lens of personal achievement and individual skill, the value of building and maintaining strong relationships with coaches, teammates, and opponents cannot be underestimated.

Interpersonal relationship with coach
In tennis, the significance of cultivating a strong interpersonal relationship with a coach cannot be understated. This bond is crucial not only for technical and tactical development but also for fostering overall well-being and performance. Effective communication stands at the core of this relationship. When players and coaches engage in open and honest dialogue, it ensures that feedback and guidance are tailored to meet individual needs. This transparent communication allows coaches to adapt their strategies to better suit a player's unique strengths and areas for improvement, enhancing the overall effectiveness of training.

Trust and credibility form the bedrock of a successful coach-player relationship. When players trust their coach, they are more inclined to fully embrace the training regimen and adhere to strategic advice. This trust fosters a deeper commitment to the coaching process, ultimately leading to better outcomes on the court. A coach who has earned a player's trust and respect can significantly influence their dedication and effort, leading to more profound improvements.

Personalized coaching is another vital aspect of this relationship. A strong bond allows coaches to understand their players on a more personal level, which is essential for tailoring advice and strategies. This personalized approach ensures that coaching methods align with a player's specific needs, whether they relate to technical skills, psychological factors, or emotional support.

Motivation and support are also critical components of a positive coach-player relationship. A coach who provides encouragement and demonstrates genuine concern for a player's success can greatly enhance their motivation and morale. This support is especially valuable during challenging times, helping players maintain a positive mindset and stay focused on their goals.

Effective conflict resolution is another benefit of a strong interpersonal relationship. Disagreements and conflicts are inevitable in any coaching scenario, but a well-established relationship allows these issues to be addressed constructively. By maintaining mutual respect and understanding, players and coaches can resolve conflicts without damaging their partnership, fostering a more productive and harmonious working environment.

Interpersonal relationships with Team mates
The importance of cultivating strong interpersonal relationships with tennis teammates and peers extends well beyond the boundaries of practice sessions and matches. Building a positive rapport with fellow players fosters a supportive and collaborative environment, which is essential for both personal and collective growth. When players develop mutual respect and trust, they create a network of encouragement and shared goals, enhancing motivation and teamwork. This camaraderie not only boosts individual confidence but also strengthens team cohesion, leading to more effective practice sessions and strategic collaboration during competitions. Furthermore, strong relationships with peers contribute to a more enjoyable and fulfilling tennis experience, as players can rely on each other for support, and constructive feedback. By nurturing these connections, players develop essential social skills, such as empathy and cooperation, which are invaluable both on and off the court, enriching their overall experience and contributing to long-term success.

Interpersonal relationships with opponents
Building positive interpersonal relationships with opponents is a crucial yet often overlooked aspect of tennis. Engaging with opponents respectfully and professionally not only enhances the sportsmanship of

the game but also opens opportunities for valuable learning and growth. Developing a rapport with opponents can lead to more insightful exchanges of tactics and techniques, offering players different perspectives that can enrich their own strategies. Such relationships foster a culture of mutual respect, transforming competitive encounters into constructive experiences rather than adversarial confrontations.

Building Interpersonal Relationship skills on the Tennis Court

Building interpersonal relationships on the tennis court involves several key practices that enhance both personal and team dynamics. To start, it's crucial to cultivate a sense of connection with teammates by engaging in regular, open communication and demonstrating a genuine interest in each other's progress and well-being. This includes providing constructive feedback, celebrating successes, and offering support during challenging times. Developing a strong rapport with your coach also requires clear, honest communication and a willingness to accept and act on feedback. This relationship is built on mutual respect and trust, which allows for effective coaching and personal growth. When it comes to interacting with opponents, maintaining professionalism and respect is paramount. Even in competitive moments, showing sportsmanship and understanding fosters a positive environment and builds mutual respect. Additionally, team-building activities, joint practice sessions, and group discussions can further strengthen relationships by enhancing understanding and cooperation among players. These practices help in creating a supportive atmosphere, which is essential for both individual and collective success.

Empathy and effective communication are fundamental life skills that significantly contribute to building and maintaining strong interpersonal relationships. Empathy allows individuals to understand and share the feelings of others, fostering deeper connections and trust. By putting yourself in someone else's shoes, you can respond more sensitively and constructively, whether it's supporting a teammate through a tough match or understanding a coach's feedback. Effective communication, on the other hand, involves clearly conveying your thoughts and feelings while actively listening to others. It ensures that misunderstandings are minimized and that everyone involved feels heard and valued. Both skills are not only vital for navigating the complexities of tennis but are also universally applicable across various life contexts. They enhance personal relationships, facilitate teamwork, and contribute to a more empathetic and communicative society. Thus, while these skills are honed on the tennis court, their benefits extend far beyond the sport, making them essential tools for success in any area of life.

In conclusion, while the principles of building interpersonal relationships detailed here are rooted in the context of tennis, their relevance extends far beyond the sport. The practices of developing connection with teammates, fostering mutual respect with coaches, and maintaining professionalism with opponents are universally applicable strategies that can enhance interpersonal connections in any setting. Whether in personal relationships, professional environments, or community interactions, the core elements of empathy, effective communication, and mutual respect play a crucial role in nurturing and sustaining meaningful connections. By applying these principles, individuals can create a supportive and collaborative atmosphere, improve their ability to work effectively with others, and foster deeper, more understanding relationships. The skills developed on the tennis court—through clear communication, empathetic interactions, and professional conduct—are transferable and invaluable in any context. They contribute to personal growth, enhance team dynamics, and improve overall relational success, demonstrating that the lessons learned from sports are not just confined to athletic endeavors but are vital for thriving in various aspects of life.

10. Coping with stress and emotion: Mastering Resilience

"As a tennis player, you have to get used to losing every week. Unless you win the tournament, you always go home as a loser. But you have to take the positive out of a defeat and go back to work. Improve to fail better".

> *- Stan Wawrinka*

Coping with stress is an essential life skill that plays a pivotal role in maintaining overall well-being and resilience in the face of life's inevitable pressures and challenges. At its core, effective stress management involves not just addressing immediate stressors, but also developing long-term strategies to handle the emotional and mental strains that arise from various aspects of life, from personal and professional responsibilities to unforeseen crises. Mastering this skill is about more than just enduring tough times; it's about learning to adapt and thrive despite them.

In a world where demands are constant and expectations are high, the ability to cope with stress enables individuals to maintain a sense of balance and perspective. It involves cultivating techniques to manage anxiety, prevent burnout, and preserve mental clarity. This skill is crucial for navigating life's challenges without becoming overwhelmed, thereby protecting both mental and physical health. Effective stress management allows individuals to approach problems with a clear mind, make reasoned decisions, and sustain their energy and motivation over time.

Understanding how to cope with stress means recognizing its sources, such as work pressures, relationship dynamics, or personal goals, and developing personalized strategies to address them. This includes not only practical approaches like time management and setting realistic goals but also fostering emotional resilience through mindfulness, relaxation techniques, and positive thinking. By mastering these skills, individuals can transform stress from a debilitating force into a manageable aspect of their lives, ultimately enhancing their ability to lead a balanced and fulfilling life.

The Significance of Coping With Stress in Tennis:

Coping with stress is an integral aspect of tennis, profoundly influencing both a player's performance on the court and their overall well-being. The significance of stress management in tennis cannot be overstated, as it directly impacts mental resilience, consistency, and long-term success in the sport.

Tennis is a mentally demanding sport that requires players to continuously bounce back from failures, setbacks, and unpredictable changes during a match. The ability to cope with stress builds mental resilience, allowing players to approach challenges with a positive mindset rather than being overwhelmed by them. This mental toughness enables players to remain focused and adapt to the ever-changing dynamics of the game, which is crucial for maintaining a competitive edge.

In high-stakes matches, where pressure is at its peak, the importance of stress management becomes even more apparent. Tennis matches often come down to a few crucial points, where the ability to perform under pressure can make the difference between victory and defeat. Players who have honed their stress-coping mechanisms are better equipped to handle these critical moments, ensuring that their performance stays strong when it matters most.

Furthermore, managing stress is essential for maintaining overall health and well-being in the sport. The rigorous demands of long tournaments, extensive travel schedules, and the relentless pressure to perform can take a toll on mental and physical health. Incorporating stress management techniques such as mindfulness, relaxation exercises, and controlled breathing can significantly reduce the adverse effects of stress. These practices not only help players maintain their composure during matches but also contribute to their longevity in the sport by preventing burnout and promoting recovery.

Consistency is another critical factor influenced by stress management. Stress can lead to fluctuations in performance, with players experiencing highs and lows throughout a match or tournament. By developing effective coping strategies, players can achieve a more stable level of play, which is critical for success in tennis. Consistency allows players to navigate the ups and downs of a match without being derailed by stress-induced errors or lapses in concentration.

Injury prevention is also closely linked to stress management. Physical tension resulting from stress can increase the likelihood of injuries, which can sideline players and disrupt their training and competition schedules. By adopting strategies that reduce stress, players can minimize physical strain and lower their risk of injury, ensuring they can perform at their best without compromising their physical health.

Beyond individual performance, stress management plays a vital role in fostering positive team dynamics, especially in team competitions like Inter-school, National, or International events. Players who can effectively manage stress contribute to a supportive and cohesive team environment, enhancing the collective performance of the group. Positive team dynamics are essential for achieving success in team-based competitions, where the performance of each member impacts the overall outcome.

The importance of coping with stress extends to the post-match recovery period as well. Players who can effectively manage the stress of competition are better equipped to recover both physically and mentally after a match. This quick recovery is crucial for preparing for subsequent matches, especially in tournaments where players may have to compete multiple times in a short span.

In the long run, adopting healthy stress-coping mechanisms can significantly prolong a player's tennis career. Those who can navigate the challenges and pressures of the sport without succumbing to excessive stress are more likely to enjoy sustained success and avoid the pitfalls of burnout or chronic injury.

Moreover, coping with stress involves mastering emotional regulation. Tennis players often experience a wide range of emotions, including frustration, disappointment, and anxiety, which can impact their decision-making and strategic play. By learning to manage these emotions effectively, players can maintain a more strategic and composed game, leading to better performance on the court.

Lastly, effective stress management enhances focus and concentration, both of which are critical for success in tennis. Stress can serve as a significant distraction, pulling a player's attention away from the task at hand. Players who develop strong coping mechanisms can maintain a high level of focus, leading to better decision-making, sharper execution of shots, and ultimately, greater success in matches.

Building Coping with Stress Skills on the Tennis Court:

Breathing Exercises
Incorporating deep breathing exercises into your pre-match routine is a foundational method for managing stress on the tennis court. By focusing on slow, controlled breaths, you can calm your nervous system, reduce anxiety, and center your mind. This practice helps you approach each point with a sense of calm and clarity, allowing you to execute your strategies without being overwhelmed by pressure.

Visualization
Visualization is a powerful tool in stress management. By mentally rehearsing successful outcomes and picturing yourself confidently handling stressful situations on the court, you reinforce a positive mindset. Visualization can enhance your focus and boost your ability to perform under pressure, making it easier to stay composed and execute precise shots during critical moments.

Mindfulness Meditation
Mindfulness meditation is another effective way to build stress-coping skills. By practicing mindfulness, you train yourself to stay present and fully engaged with each point, rather than dwelling on past mistakes or worrying about future challenges. This heightened awareness helps you maintain focus and composure, even in high-pressure situations.

Pre-Point and Post-Point Routines
Establishing consistent pre-point and post-point routines creates a sense of control and stability on the court. These routines help you manage stress by providing a structured approach to each point, allowing you to reset and refocus after every play. This consistency is key to maintaining a steady mindset during critical moments in a match.

Positive Self-Talk
Cultivating positive self-talk is essential for building mental resilience. By replacing negative thoughts with affirmations and constructive internal dialogue, you can reinforce confidence and maintain focus. Positive self-talk helps you stay motivated and resilient, even when facing difficult challenges or setbacks on the court.

Pressure Simulation During Practice
Simulating high-pressure scenarios during practice is a crucial strategy for building stress-coping skills. By creating match-like conditions that test your ability to handle stress, you become more familiar with the pressures of competition. This familiarity helps you develop effective coping mechanisms, making it easier to stay composed and perform well under stress during actual matches.

Adaptability Training
Adaptability training involves practicing quick adjustments to changing circumstances on the court. This type of training enhances your ability to cope with stress by preparing you to handle the unpredictability of real match situations. Being adaptable allows you to stay flexible and resilient, no matter what challenges arise during a match.

Post-Match Reflection
Reflecting on your performance after a match is an important part of
building stress-coping skills. By analyzing how well you managed stress
during competition, you can identify areas for improvement and develop
targeted strategies for future matches. Post-match reflection helps you
learn from your experiences and continually refine your stress
management techniques.

Building Coping with Emotions Skills on the Tennis Court

1.Self-Awareness:
Begin by recognizing and acknowledging your emotions. Whether it's
excitement, frustration, or nervousness, understanding what you feel is
the first step to effective coping.

2.Pre-Match Rituals:
Develop pre-match rituals that help create a calm and focused mindset.
This could include visualization, deep breathing exercises, or a few
minutes of mindfulness to center yourself before stepping onto the court.

3.Mind-Body Connection:
Train your mind and body to work together. Connect your emotional
state with physical
cues. For instance, associate deep breaths with calming nerves or a
specific mantra with boosting confidence.

4.Positive Affirmations:
Arm yourself with positive affirmations. Create a list of statements that
resonate with you and boost your morale. Repeat these affirmations
during challenging moments to shift your mindset.
> 1. "I am focused, present, and ready to give my best on the
> court."
> 2. "Every match is an opportunity to showcase my skills and
> enjoy the game."
> 3. "I trust in my training and believe in my ability to handle any
> challenge."

4. "With every point, I am growing as a player and becoming stronger."
5. "I am resilient; setbacks are stepping stones to success in my tennis journey."
6. "My mind is clear, and I make wise decisions under pressure."
7. "I embrace the joy of competition and celebrate both victories and lessons."
8. "I am in control of my reactions, staying calm and composed during matches."
9. "Every serve, every volley, and every shot I take is a step toward improvement."
10. "I am grateful for the opportunity to play tennis, and I approach each match with gratitude."

5.Embrace Setbacks as Opportunities:
Instead of viewing setbacks as failures, see them as opportunities for growth. Analyze what went wrong objectively, learn from it, and use the experience to improve your game.

6.Focus on What You Can Control:
 Tennis is full of variables, but focus on what you can control—your mindset, effort, and reactions. Letting go of factors beyond your control minimizes stress and helps you stay in the zone.

7.Healthy Outlets for Emotions:
 Establish healthy outlets for your emotions. Whether it's discussing your feelings with a coach, journaling, or even a brief moment of solitude, finding constructive ways to express emotions is key.

8.Realistic Goal Setting:
Set realistic and achievable goals. While ambition is commendable, setting attainable milestones prevents unnecessary pressure and reduces the intensity of emotions during play.

9.Mindful Breathing during Play:
Incorporate mindful breathing during the match. Take intentional breaths between points to maintain composure and reset your focus. Controlled breathing can be a game-changer in managing on-court emotions.

10.Post-Match Reflection:
After the match, reflect on your emotional responses. What worked? What didn't? This self-reflection is invaluable for continuous improvement and refining your coping mechanisms.

11.Seek Guidance:
Don't hesitate to seek guidance from coaches, sports psychologists, or mentors. They can provide tailored strategies to help you cope with specific emotional challenges.

Unlocking Excellence: A Guide to Visualisation in Tennis –
Learn and Apply My Personal Practice Routine:

Visualisation, also known as mental imagery is a powerful technique that
involves creating a detailed mental picture of a desired outcome. Here, I
am sharing how I do visualisation practice so you can also effectively
practice it every day or before going to a match.

1. Quiet and Calm Environment:
Find a quiet and comfortable space where you won't be disturbed. This
could be a quiet
room or a peaceful spot on the tennis court.

2. Close Your Eyes:
Close your eyes to eliminate external distractions and allow your mind to
turn inward.

3. Relaxation Techniques:
Start by taking a 8 deep breaths to relax your body and mind. You can
use either 4-7-8 breathing technique (Breath-in in the counts of 4, hold
your breathe on the count of 7 and breath-out in the count of 8) or 4-4-4
breathing technique (Breath-in in the count of 4, hold your breathe on the
count of 4, breath-out in the count of 4 and hold your breathe in the count
of 4). Relaxation techniques can help create a focused and receptive state
for visualisation.

4. Choose a Specific Scenario:
Select a specific scenario related to tennis that you want to visualise. It
could be executing a perfect serve, making a crucial return, or handling a
stressful situation with composure.

5. Create a Vivid Image:
Imagine the scenario as vividly as possible. Picture yourself on the tennis
court, the feel of the racquet in your hand, the sounds of the
surroundings, and the details of your opponent and the environment.

6. Engage All Senses:
Engage multiple senses in your visualisation. Feel the texture of the
tennis ball, hear the sound of the ball hitting the strings, and sense the
movement of your body as you execute each shot.

7. Positive Emotions:
Associate positive emotions with the visualisation. Feel the joy of
success, the confidence in your abilities, and the satisfaction of a well-
executed play.

8. Repetition:
Repeat the visualisation several times. Repetition helps reinforce the
mental image and enhances its impact on your subconscious mind.

9. Include Challenges:
Integrate challenging situations into your visualisation. Imagine facing a
tough opponent, being a few points behind, and successfully navigating
these challenges with resilience and skill.

10. Variety of Scenarios:
Visualise a variety of scenarios to cover different aspects of your game.
Include scenarios from different matches, various playing conditions, and
diverse opponents.

11. Consistency is Key:
Make visualisation a consistent part of your mental training routine.
Regular practice enhances its effectiveness over time.

12. Combine with Physical Practice:
Use visualisation as a complement to your physical practice. Imagine
yourself practising specific techniques or strategies that you are currently
working on.

13. Post-Visualisation Reflection:
After each session, reflect on how the visualisation made you feel and the details you were able to imagine. This reflection reinforces the positive aspects of your mental imagery.

14. Adapt to Match Conditions:
Visualise scenarios that align with actual match conditions. Imagine the pressure, crowd noise, and competitive atmosphere to enhance realism.

15. Believe in the Outcome:
Develop a sense of belief in the positive outcomes you visualise. The more you believe in your ability to succeed, the more likely you are to translate these mental images into on-court success.

Mindfulness practise i use to stay present during a tennis match

Pre-Point Routine:
Before each point, take a moment to stand comfortably, close your eyes
briefly, and take a deep breath. Inhale positivity and exhale any tension.

 Focus on Breath:
As you step up to the baseline, pay attention to your breath. Inhale
deeply, feeling the air filling your lungs, and exhale, releasing any stress
or distractions.

Court Awareness:
Look around and notice the details of the court—the color of the lines,
the feel of the surface under your shoes. This helps anchor you to the
present moment.

Mindful Ball Bounce:
During your opponent's serve or when waiting for your turn, focus on the
bounce of the ball. Watch it attentively, tracking its movement and
height.

Let Go of Past and Future:
If a previous point didn't go as planned or you're thinking about the next
one, gently redirect your mind to the current point. Remind yourself that
each point is a new opportunity.

Breathing Between Points:
Use the moments between points to practice mindful breathing. Inhale as
you walk to the baseline, exhale as you prepare for the next serve or
return.

Ground Yourself:
Feel the ground beneath your feet. Be aware of the connection between your body and the court. This grounds you in the present and enhances stability.

Sensory Awareness:
Engage your senses. Listen to the sound of the ball, feel the vibration in your racket, and observe the surroundings. This sensory awareness keeps you in the 'now.'

Reset with Mindful Timeout:
If a point doesn't go your way, take a mindful timeout. Step back, breathe deeply, and let go of any frustration or disappointment before the next point.

Overcoming pre-match anxiety by mindfully engaging five senses

1. Sight:

Pre-Match Visualisation: Before the match, visualize yourself playing confidently and successfully. Picture precise serves, accurate shots, and victorious moments. This positive imagery can help build confidence and reduce anxiety.

Court Awareness: During the match, focus on the visual details of the court—observe the colors, the lines, and the overall environment. This anchors you to the present moment and minimizes anxious thoughts about the past or future.

2. Hearing:

Breathing Rhythm: Pay attention to the sound of your breath. Establish a steady breathing rhythm, inhaling and exhaling deliberately. This not only calms your nervous system but also helps maintain focus during crucial points.

Ball Impact: Listen to the sound of the ball hitting the racket. This auditory cue can keep you grounded and connected to the current point, reducing anxiety about the overall match outcome.

3. Touch:

Grounding Techniques: Feel the texture of the tennis court under your shoes. During breaks or timeouts, take a moment to stand still, feel the ground beneath you, and connect with the earth. This grounding technique helps center your focus and alleviate anxiety.

Racket Grip Awareness: Be aware of the sensation in your hands as you hold the racket. Adjust your grip during breaks, and consciously feel the pressure and texture. This tactile awareness keeps you in the present moment.

4. Smell:

Scented Breathing: Incorporate aromatherapy into your pre-match routine. Inhale calming scents like lavender or chamomile before stepping onto the court. Associating a specific smell with relaxation can ease anxiety and create a positive mental state.

5. Taste:

Hydration Ritual: Maintain hydration with water or a drink. Take deliberate sips during breaks, focusing on the taste and temperature. This simple act of mindfulness redirects your attention from anxious thoughts to the present physical experience.

Example Scenario:

Before a match, find a quiet spot to sit. Close your eyes and take a few deep breaths. Inhale a calming scent (lavender or a favorite aroma). As you breathe, visualise the upcoming match, focusing on successful plays. Open your eyes, feel the ground under you, listen to the surrounding sounds, and take a sip of water, savoring the taste. This sensory experience helps center your mind and reduce match-related anxiety.

Sharpening Focus: The One-Point Focus Drill for Enhanced Concentration on the Tennis Court

Steps to practise One-Point Focus Drill:

1. Choose a Focal Point:

Select a small and specific point on the tennis court. It could be a part of the net, a line, or a particular spot on the opponent's side.

2. Pre-Point Routine:

Before each point, as part of your routine, consciously fixate your gaze on the chosen focal point. Take a moment to clear your mind and direct your attention to that single spot.

3. Maintain Focus During Points:

As the point begins, keep your eyes locked on the chosen point. Regardless of the ball's movement or your opponent's actions, make a concerted effort to maintain your gaze on that spot.

4. Return to Focus Between Points:

During breaks or timeouts, return your focus to the chosen point. This helps reset your concentration for the upcoming points and prevents distractions.

5. Challenge Yourself Gradually:

Start with this drill during practice sessions or friendly matches. As you become more comfortable, gradually incorporate it into competitive situations.

6. Mindful Breathing:

Combine the drill with mindful breathing. Inhale deeply as you fixate on the focal point, and exhale any tension or distractions. This synchronization enhances both focus and relaxation.

7. Expand Awareness:

Over time, expand your awareness to include peripheral vision while keeping the primary focus. This broader awareness helps you stay engaged with the entire court while maintaining a central point of focus.

8. Review and Adjust:

After each practice session or match, reflect on your performance using this technique. Adjust your focal point or breathing techniques based on what enhances your focus the most.

Benefits:

1. Enhanced Concentration: By consistently focusing on a single point, you strengthen your ability to concentrate during high-pressure situations.

2. Reduced Distractions: The drill helps minimize distractions, allowing you to stay mentally composed and attentive during each point.

3. Improved Visual Tracking: Sharpening your visual tracking skills contributes to better anticipation and decision-making on the court.

Mastering Concentration: The Point-by-Point Mindfulness Technique for Peak Performance in Tennis"

1. Pre-Point Routine:

Develop a consistent pre-point routine. This can include bouncing the ball a specific number of times, adjusting your strings, or taking a deep breath. This routine signals your brain that it's time to focus on the upcoming point.

2. Breathe and Center:

Before each point, take a deep breath. Inhale slowly, hold for a moment, and exhale completely. This brief moment of conscious breathing helps center your mind and brings your attention to the present.

3. Focus on Your Opponent:

As you prepare for the point, look at your opponent. Pay attention to their body language, stance, and positioning on the court. This helps you anticipate their moves and stay actively engaged in the point.

4. Visualise Success:

Envision a successful outcome for the upcoming point. Picture yourself executing the perfect serve, making accurate shots, and ultimately winning the point. Positive visualization enhances confidence and directs your focus toward success.

5. Single-Point Focus:

During the point, concentrate solely on the current action. Avoid dwelling on past mistakes or thinking about future points. Your attention should be fully directed to the ball, your opponent, and your strategic moves.

6. Reactive, Not Reactive:

React to the ball and your opponent's actions in real-time. Instead of worrying about the overall score or the outcome of the match, focus on responding effectively to each shot and situation as it unfolds.

7. Mindful Reset:

After each point, win or lose, take a moment to reset. Use your pre-point routine, take another deep breath, and let go of any lingering thoughts from the previous point. This brief reset prepares you for the next point with a clear mind.

8. Stay in the Present:

Continuously remind yourself to stay in the present moment. If your mind starts to wander or if you find yourself getting distracted, gently bring your focus back to the ongoing point.

9. Post-Point Analysis:

Save detailed analysis for practice sessions. During a match, keep post-point reflections brief and constructive. Use them to adjust your strategy for the next point rather than dwelling on what has passed.

10. Consistent Practice:

Incorporate this mindfulness technique into both practice sessions and actual matches. The more consistently you apply it, the more natural and effective it becomes.

11. Closing Chapter: "Luv-All 0-0"

As we conclude our captivating journey through the world of tennis and life skills, it's time to reflect on the invaluable lessons we've learned and how they align with the World Health Organization's ten essential life skills. "Luv-All 0-0," the symbolic score that marks the beginning of every point and every opportunity, encapsulates the essence of our transformative exploration.

1. Self-Awareness (0-0): Just as every point starts with the score at "love," our journey began with self-awareness—understanding our strengths and areas for growth, both on and off the court. It serves as the foundation for improvement.

2. Communication (15-0): Like the score progressing to "15," effective communication played a pivotal role. Whether with ourselves, our coaches, or fellow players, communication created a harmonious flow, much like the rhythm of a well-played match.

3. Decision-Making (30-30): As the score reached "30," decision-making became crucial. Choosing the right shots, strategies, and responses mirrored the strategic choices made on the court, contributing to our overall success.

4. Problem Solving (40-30): Approaching the score of "40," problem-solving emerged as a vital skill. Just as players strategise to win points, we navigated challenges, analysed setbacks, and devised solutions for sustained growth.

5. Critical Thinking (Game Point): The game point represents the culmination of skills. Critical thinking guided us through intricate situations, fostering a deep understanding of the game and enabling us to triumph in decisive moments.

6. Interpersonal Relationships (Deuce): Much like the score returning to "deuce," interpersonal relationships played a cyclical role. Building connections, resolving conflicts, and cooperating with teammates contributed to our overall well-being.

7. Coping with Emotions (Advantage): In moments of advantage, emotions can sway the game. Learning to manage emotions, bounce back from setbacks, and maintain composure elevated our mental game, ensuring sustained success.

8. Coping with Stress (Deuce): Deuce, again, representing the culmination of efforts, highlighted the importance of coping with stress. Through mindfulness, resilience, and mental strength, we faced match points with grace and determination.

9. Creativity (Game point): The game point, a critical juncture, paralleled the significance of creativity. Unleashing innovative approaches and embracing the unexpected allowed us to redefine the game and find new pathways to success.

10. Coping with Emotions (Game): Finally, Game, the ultimate goal, epitomised coping with emotions Just as in tennis, life is a series of matches, and the ability to navigate the spectrum of emotions defines our journey.

As we close the chapter on "Luv-All 0-0," let us carry these life skills forward, not just in tennis but in every aspect of our lives. May the score always reset to "love," reminding us of the endless opportunities for growth and success? "Luv-All 0-0" is not just a score; it's a mindset, a philosophy, and a celebration of the continuous journey of learning, thriving, and enjoying the game of tennis and life.